TRAINS

ALE DES CHEMINS DE FER BELGES

GREAT NORTHERN

Contents

When railways first began, a steam locomotive was a thing of magic and wonder — as exciting and interesting as a spaceship is today.

Introduction

Gradually trains became part of everyday life and the subject of

stories, folk songs, and popular ballads. Generations of children grew up wanting to become engine drivers.

Even today in the age of motor cars, aeroplanes, and space travel, trains are *just* as exciting!

The Time before Railways

When people discovered the power of machines, their lives changed for ever.

Machines created industries and jobs, and the whole pace of life quickened. The old methods of transport by road and on water were no longer good enough.

Steel and steam came together and created railways.

Rail tracks were not a new idea. An English engineer, George Stephenson, worked at a coalmine where trucks of coal were pulled along tracks. His job was to look after a steam engine, which pumped water from the mine.

He often wondered if the engine could also be made to pull trucks along rails. In 1814, he built a steam locomotive that was as powerful as forty horses. Eleven years later, while working as an engineer on the Stockton and Darlington Railway, he built a locomotive which pulled the first train on the line. It was called

6

Locomotion, and it could haul more than thirty wagons.

Stephenson's most famous locomotive was *Rocket*, which won a competition for steam locomotives by reaching a top speed of 48 kph (30 mph).

He also designed and built the world's first public railway, between Liverpool and Manchester, in England. When the line opened in 1830, the railway age had begun. Three months later, a railway was opened in the United States, and soon railways were being built all over the world.

7

Tens of thousands of men laboured to build the railways, working only with picks, shovels, and wheelbarrows. They lived in rough, uncomfortable camps that moved along the lines as they were built. It was dangerous work, and many died in accidents with gunpowder and falling rocks and earth.

Great rivers and valleys were spanned by spectacular bridges and viaducts. Some lines climbed over mountain ranges, others tunnelled through them. Each line produced new engineering wonders and achievements. It was all done by hand — there were no machines.

Building the Railways

In the old-world countries of Europe, railways were built from town to town, often following age-old trade routes; while in young countries such as America, the railways went like pioneers out into the wilderness.

Jungfraujoch

Carlisle R

EWCASTLE STATION on the Morn

day, Ju

gers at all the Stations; who may r
d of July. Parties from North Shiel
orning of July 1.

owcastle to Carlisle a

1S. Second
Class, 8s. 6d

9

Everywhere the railway went the local station became a place of great importance.

Many city stations were large buildings with steel and glass roofs over lots of tracks and platforms. A country station would be quite small, but no less important to the community it served. Beside the station were the goods yards, busy with rows of wagons.

Because of the railway, the townsfolk now enjoyed a speedy mail service. There was fresh food brought in every day from the country. For the first time, people of inland towns could eat fresh fish from the sea.

The Railway Station

To make it all possible, the railways employed thousands of workers.

Railway time became the correct time by which everybody set their clocks. 11

When railways first began, it was a novelty to take a train ride.

Very soon trains took people to work every day, and brought them back again to homes that could now be built out in suburbs away from the old and crowded city centres.

Trains took townspeople on excursions.

As the rails spread across continents, journeys could take many days.

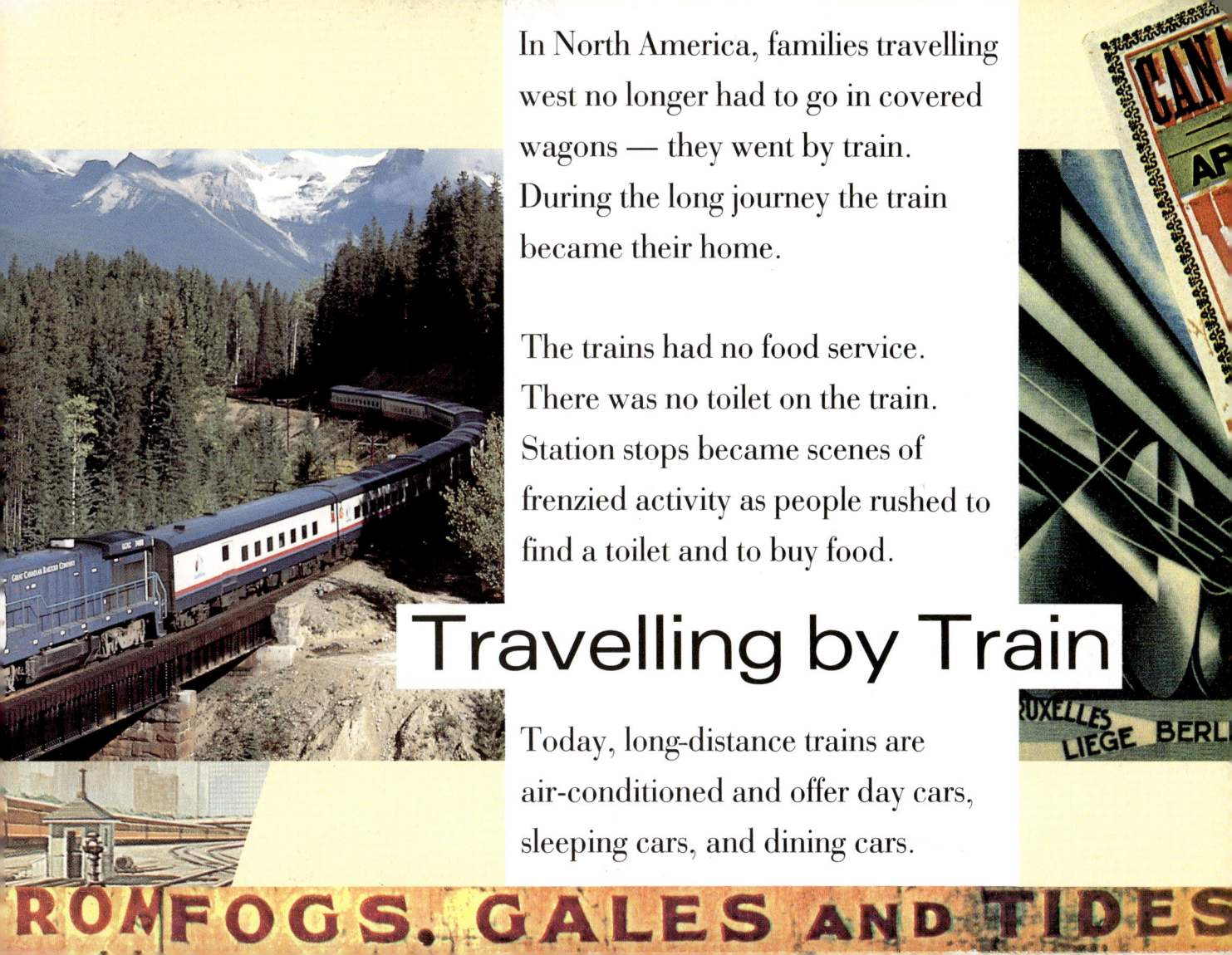

In North America, families travelling west no longer had to go in covered wagons — they went by train. During the long journey the train became their home.

The trains had no food service. There was no toilet on the train. Station stops became scenes of frenzied activity as people rushed to find a toilet and to buy food.

Travelling by Train

Today, long-distance trains are air-conditioned and offer day cars, sleeping cars, and dining cars.

It was some time before the railways became as safe as they are now. At first, there were no proper signals. Policemen stood by the track with flags!

Semaphore signals on tall posts, controlled from signal boxes, brough safety to the lines.

Safety on the Line

The signalman set the signals and track points by pulling heavy levers. The telegraph told him when the track was clear for a train to proceed.

Today's trains are guided by coloured light signals controlled from a computerized central traffic office, where one operator can safely guide trains over hundreds of kilometres of track.

The Locomotives

In nearly 2000 years of history, no one had ever travelled faster than a horse could gallop. Trains changed all that.

Opponents of the very early railways had tried to frighten people by warning of terrible sicknesses that could strike them down if they allowed themselves to be carried along at dangerous speeds. People took no notice. They wanted to travel, and they wanted speed. The trains gave them both.

The first steam locomo[tive] may have looked like teakettles on wheels, but they quickly developed into machines of great power.

They could be dirty and difficult to work on, but they hauled the world's trains for over 125 years. Today's trains are pulled by clean, efficient diesel and electric locomotives, travelling at speeds undreamed of in the days of Stephenson's *Rocket*.

...ains and railways have become famous and are a part of railway history and legend.

...e of the most famous trains is the *Orient Express*. Originally its journey took it right
...ross Europe, from Paris to Istanbul. Because it crossed many international borders,
there grew around it many stories of intrigue, spying, and adventure. Today's
Venice Simplon-Orient Express, running between London and Venice, is the most
luxurious train in the world.

Famous Trains and Railways

Some trains have become famous for their speed. The *Royal Scot* and the *Flying Scotsman* competed with each other to provide the fastest service between London and Scotland.

Everyone has heard of Japan's "bullet" trains. They took railways a big step forward. They have shown the technology and shape of trains to come.

The highest railway in the world crosses the Andes mountains in Peru and climbs to almost 4,900 m (16,000 ft). The trains have to be fitted with oxygen supplies in case passengers are taken ill with altitude sickness.

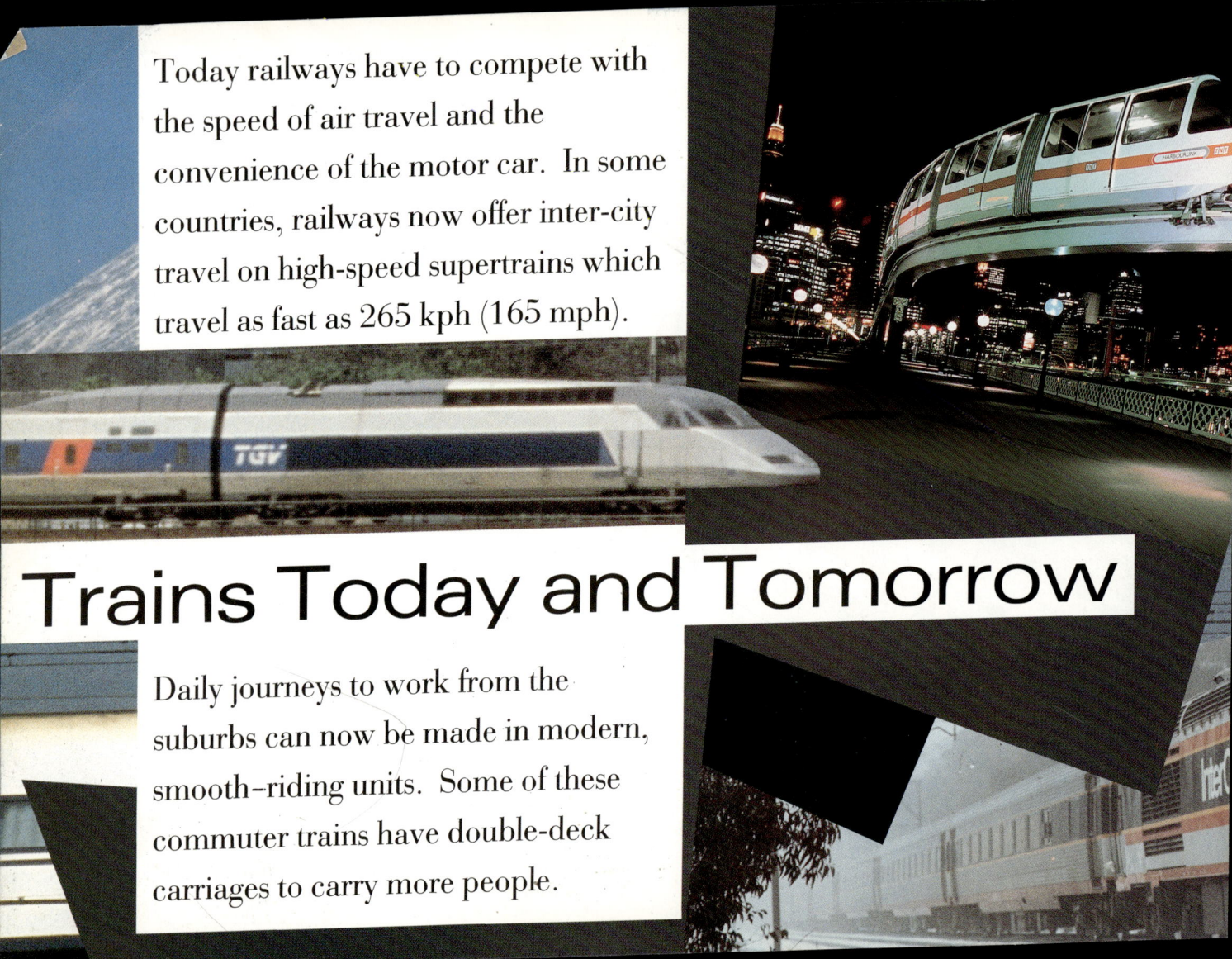

Today railways have to compete with the speed of air travel and the convenience of the motor car. In some countries, railways now offer inter-city travel on high-speed supertrains which travel as fast as 265 kph (165 mph).

Trains Today and Tomorrow

Daily journeys to work from the suburbs can now be made in modern, smooth–riding units. Some of these commuter trains have double-deck carriages to carry more people.

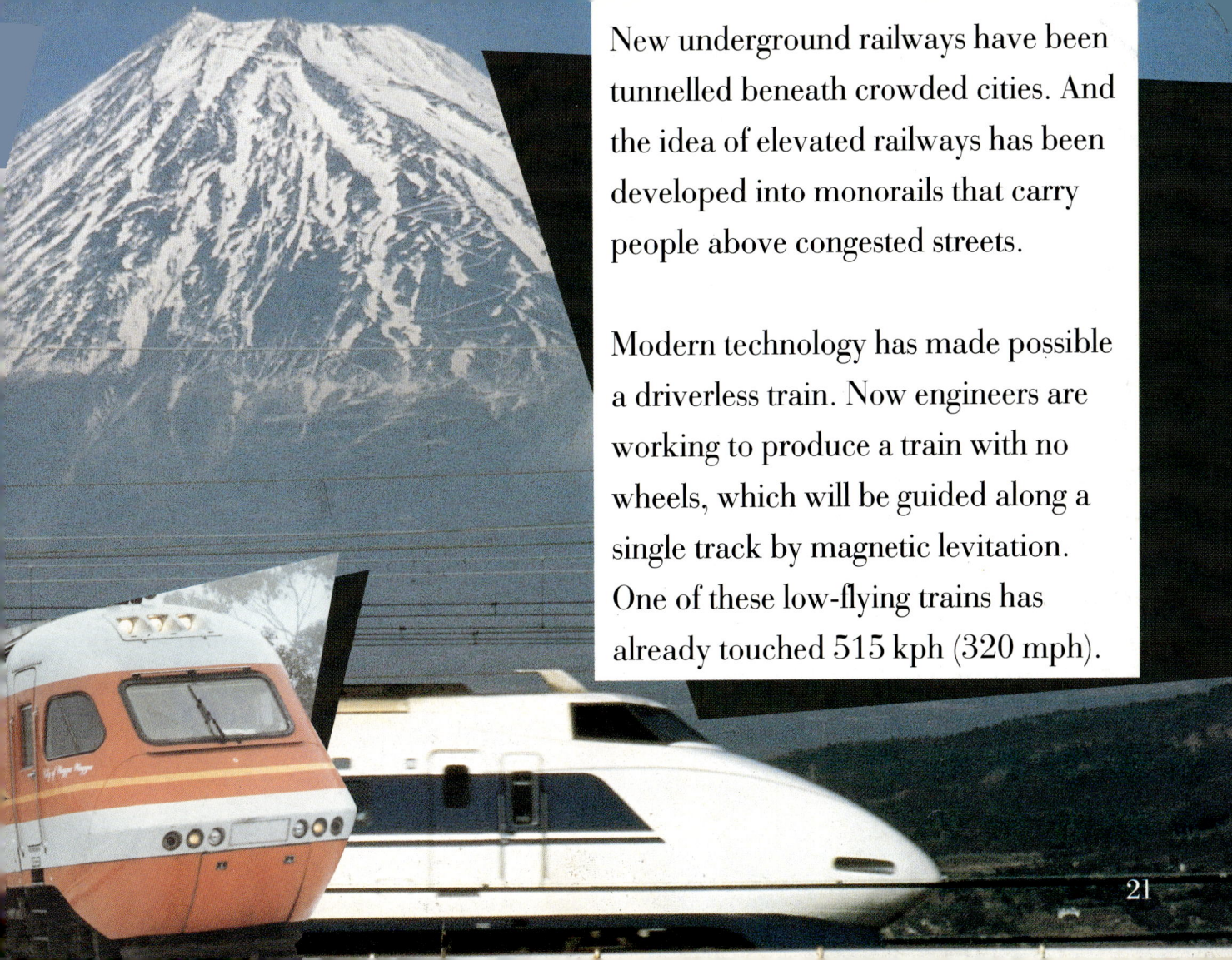

New underground railways have been tunnelled beneath crowded cities. And the idea of elevated railways has been developed into monorails that carry people above congested streets.

Modern technology has made possible a driverless train. Now engineers are working to produce a train with no wheels, which will be guided along a single track by magnetic levitation. One of these low-flying trains has already touched 515 kph (320 mph).

Around the world, museums have been created to preserve our railway history. Old and famous steam locomotives have become treasures on display to the public. There are also special working steam railways, where children can discover, and adults remember, something of how railways used to be.

Steam trains occasionally travel on the modern main line, and the sight and sound of these living machines attract crowds of people wherever they go.

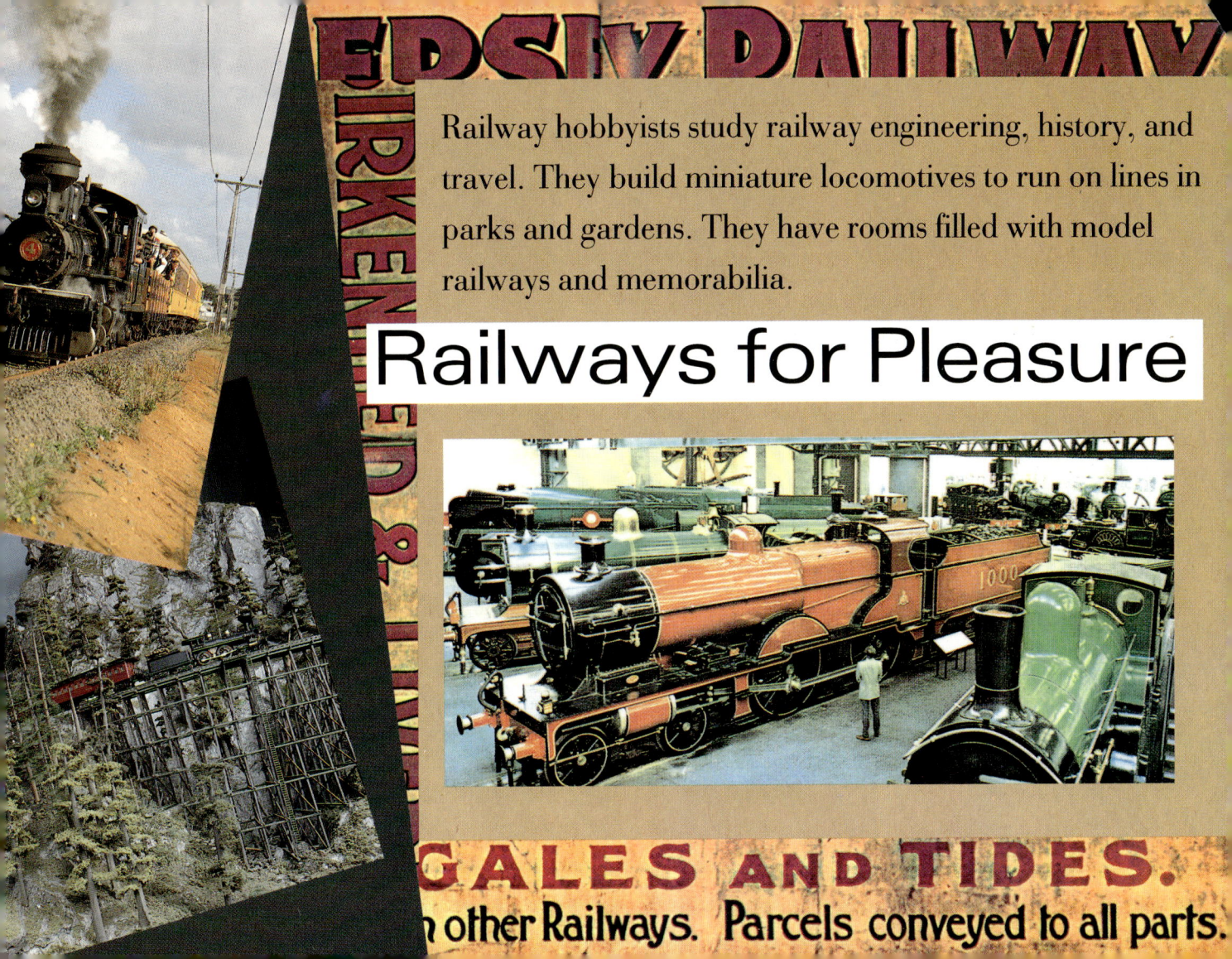

Railway hobbyists study railway engineering, history, and travel. They build miniature locomotives to run on lines in parks and gardens. They have rooms filled with model railways and memorabilia.

Railways for Pleasure

There will always be those who find trains and railways exciting and interesting!